Questions
to Bring You
Closer to

Grandma &
Grandpa

Stuart Gustafson

adamsmedia
Avon, Massachusetts

Published by Adams Media,
an F+W Publications Company
57 Littlefield Street
Avon, MA 02322
www.adamsmedia.com

ISBN-10: 1-59869-480-4
ISBN-13: 978-1-59869-480-2

Printed in the United States of America.

J I H G F E D C B A

Library of Congress Cataloging-in-Publication Data
is available from the publisher.

This publication is designed to provide accurate and authoritative information with regard to the subject matter covered. It is sold with the understanding that the publisher is not engaged in rendering legal, accounting, or other professional advice. If legal advice or other expert assistance is required, the services of a competent professional person should be sought.
—From a *Declaration of Principles* jointly adopted by a Committee of the American Bar Association and a Committee of Publishers and Associations

Many of the designations used by manufacturers and sellers to distinguish their products are claimed as trademarks. Where those designations appear in this book and Adams Media was aware of a trademark claim, the designations have been printed with initial capital letters.

This book is available at quantity discounts for bulk purchases.
For information, please call 1-800-289-0963.

From Stuart Gustafson—I wish to dedicate this book to all the grandparents who are so excited by the sight and the sounds of their precious grandchildren. I never really knew my grandparents. My mom's father had died at an early age, and her mother passed away when I was eleven. My dad's father was killed in the same car crash that killed my dad when I was sixteen; and I did not have the chance to know his mom because we moved a lot when I was young—Dad was in the U.S. Navy. Being able to spend time with loving grandparents was a piece of life that I missed out on, and so I try to make up for it by spending time with my own loving family. Therefore, I give special thanks to my wife Darlene, and to our children, Adrianne and Woodrow. I consider myself to be truly blessed to have Robyn Freedman Spizman as my coauthor.

From Robyn Spizman—To my parents, Phyllis and Jack Freedman, who have shared with me the joy of the generations past and celebrated the goal of preserving the special memories we all hold near and dear to our hearts. And to my husband, Willy, and our children, Justin and Ali, who make my life so worthwhile and create new memories that sustain me. And to Doug and Genie Freedman, Sam and Gena Spizman, Aunt Lois and Uncle Jerry, Aunt Ramona, and to my real life angel, Betty Storne, and The Spizman Agency, Jenny Corsey, my family and friends, too numerous to mention, you are permanently recorded in my mind and heart forever. To my grandparents, who no longer grace the earth, you wholeheartedly grace my spirit daily.

contents

acknowledgments

Once again we have been fortunate to have the support of the professional staff of Adams Media to guide us through the process of planning, writing, and editing. We want to particularly thank Karen Cooper, Director of Marketing; Beth Gissinger, Director of Publicity; Paula Munier, Acquisitions Editor, and Sara Stock, Project Manager. We are also very privileged to have the professional expertise of a fantastic agent—we extend our thanks to Meredith Bernstein for her advice and assistance. And, finally, we wish to acknowledge the excellent work of Willy Spizman, Jenny Corsey, and the award-winning Spizman Agency (*www.spizmanagency.com*) for the help they have given us along with their many talents and publicity efforts promoting our books, and especially the *Questions to Bring You Closer* series.

Foreword

Grandparents are the luckiest people in the world. They get to spend time with their grandchildren, buy presents for them, spoil them, and be loved by them. Can anyone think of a better job than that? The role of a grandparent doesn't pay anything, but its rewards are immeasurable. Close your eyes and picture this—young grandchildren laughing and playing with smiling and energetic grandparents. Can't you just hear the laughter, the squeals, and the happiness that surrounds all of them? This is such a beautiful image.

However, not all grandchildren know that much about their grandparents. Just as we are all someone's son or daughter, each of us is also a grandson or a granddaughter. The difference is that not everyone is fortunate to live close to his or her grandparents; or perhaps the grandparents are deceased. It is certainly quite a loss that not all grandparents can spend precious time with their grandchildren. And it is equally a loss for anyone who is not able to know and enjoy happy times with his or her grandparents.

While the books in our *Questions to Bring You Closer* series first focused on Dad and Mom—this book on Grandma and Grandpa approaches the questions in a slightly different manner. Activities, dreams, and goals of people two generations apart are not as similar as they are between the parent-child generations. Knowing more information about your grandparents is important because your grandparents shaped your parents, and they, of course, shaped you. Who knows—learning about your grandparents might even answer some of the questions that you have had about your own parents. Whatever your personal journey is in life, we wish you meaningful moments and the ability to feel closer to those you love.

Stuart Gustafson
Boise, Idaho

Robyn Freedman Spizman
Atlanta, Georgia

Part 1

How to Use This Book

"How to Use This Book"

IF YOU ASK ADULTS to tell you their images of their grandparents, the answers will vary greatly. Some might describe a grandfather as an older man with glasses who has some gray hair. He always has a story to tell, and he'll occasionally tell you something about your dad that your dad never told you. He might not be very adept at computer skills, but he can make almost anything out of nothing. If you want to play catch, he'll play catch with you. If you want to fly a kite, he'll show you how to keep that kite flying even when there is very little breeze. Words to describe him would be "gentle," "easy-going," and "fun to be around." Others might say, "My Grandpa is an amazing runner, and he is one of the most physically fit people I know!"

The description of a grandmother would range from the grandmothers on the go, who are either involved in the community or busy at work, to the image of a grandmother who always has cookies coming out of the oven. Having unexpected company is never a problem because she can make anyone feel like an invited guest. The garden is always green with vegetables, and flowers are cut and put in various rooms in the house. As a child, you could always sit on Grandma's lap and tell her your problems—from the story behind a scraped knee to an unrequited crush on a neighborhood boy. Grandma was the "rock" of the family—the stabilizing force who made all things seem calm and peaceful.

Not all grandparents may fit the descriptions above, but we are all special and different in our own ways. Our grandparents are the piece of the family story that seems more like heritage than the stories of our own parents. After all, parents are parents, but grandparents are special. They are the ones to tell us what it was like "back then." They are not as concerned about the daily activities around our growing up—isn't that what parents are for? Grandparents are a gift to us to be more like friends than family. They will show you how to do things that parents would never do, and they are always happy to see you. Of course, you are always happy to see them because they are "fun."

Your grandparents are also a great source of information about your parents, specifically the parent whose side the grandparents are. You will be able to find out so much more about your dad from his parents than he will ever tell you on his own. If you work your dad's folks enough, they will tell about the times he was in more trouble than you've been in. He might let you think he was a star student, but your grandparents will tell you truth about his grades. And your mom? Her parents will tell you about the times she'd come home late from a date and "try" to sneak into the house. They heard her, of course, but they let her think she made it in quietly. Your grandparents can be a great source of family treasures; it would be a tremendous shame not to mine that mother lode of information.

Did you ever spend a summer with your grandparents? Was it a more relaxing atmosphere than during the school year at home? Maybe you still got up early during that summer, but it was because you were helping out on the farm, or you were headed out on a daylong activity. A lot of grandparents live in the city, and some of them are in apartment houses, but they still had a lot of activities planned for you. If you were not an avid reader during the school year, you probably read a few books during the summer because your grandparents made it fun to read. Think back to the great times you had with your grandma and grandpa; those are the feelings that you want to capture in words that you can have forever.

If you are able to sit down with your grandparents, or call and exchange e-mails with them, you should consider yourself to be a lucky person. It should not come as a surprise that not everyone has living grandparents. According to the U.S. Census Bureau, almost 67.5 million of 73.5 million children do not have living grandparents. That's a staggering 91.75 percent of children without any grandparents, and only 8.25 percent of children with any living grandparents at all—either both grandparents, or even just a grandfather or a grandmother. If you do have living grandparents—one or both—your life has truly been blessed. Or, perhaps you are a grandparent yourself, and you decided to fill out this book and later present it to your grandchildren—we think that's absolutely wonderful. Our goal is to provide an avenue so that all grandparent can not only leave memories of their heartfelt love, but also a legacy of loving thoughts, ideas, and beliefs expressed for generations to come.

On another note, if your grandparents are no longer alive, we hope to offer our support and quietly console you by providing a special way to bring their most special attributes and memories to light. We allow the memories of our grandparents to live on by carrying those special times we shared with them in our hearts and in our daily actions. With the help of this book, and through your family and individuals who knew them, the answers are still possible to obtain, if you make the time and pursue the questions. Let this information and the content you gather be a legacy of love to forever treasure.

Questions to Bring You Closer to Grandma & Grandpa was designed to help you take charge of the present and preserve the past—so you can preserve your grandparents' legacy today and not have any regrets tomorrow. The questions will guide you along a very sentimental journey as you lovingly collect memories directly from them or through friends and family who knew them. While each of our personal experiences and life experiences differ, we are connected by our need to be loved and to honor our loved ones in meaningful ways. This book will be a labor of love as you explore the times from two generations ago and reflect on how you have been shaped by them.

From our collective experiences, we believe this book will become a powerful gift you can give to yourself and to those you love. Spending time with a loved one is one of life's most precious gifts, but how many times have we taken this for granted? How many times have we wished we could go back and relive a special moment or recall a conversation? And how many times have we wasted meaningful hours focusing on things that are really not that important?

This book is an opportunity to preserve those special moments, traits, and qualities about your grandparents, the ones they hold near and dear in their hearts. If your grandparents are no longer with you, it will be a journey to discover the answers from the individuals who knew them best. Let this book guide you to a richer under-standing of the family members you call Grandma and Grandpa and keep their memories close to your heart, now and always.

We begin with a section called "What Grandma enjoys to keep her busy," and "What do you think of first when you think of Grandpa?" detailing nine different "Grandma activities" and nine different "Grandpa traits." When you find the types that fit best, you can refer to the accompanying questions as a way to begin conversation. These are the easier questions to ask, so you want to start with them.

We organized this book to assist you in documenting the details of your grandparents' lives. Our goal is to help you provide a legacy that will forever serve as a written record. The pages following these sections provide a thoughtful set of questions to ignite a conversation about the following topics:

- On Grandma and Grandpa's Lives
- On Our Family History
- On Grandma and Grandpa's Values
- On Marriage and Relationships
- On Grandma and Grandpa's Dreams and Goals
- On Children, Parenting, and Being a Grandparent
- On Grandma and Grandpa's Legacies
- Who Knows Grandma and Grandpa Best
- Grandma and Grandpa's Favorite Things

The first seven sections will help you develop the loving and lasting legacy of Grandma and Grandpa. The last two will help you gather more information about what was near and dear to them— people they knew, where they liked to go, and what they liked to do. Before you begin, share with your Grandma or Grandpa each of these sections and the topics you'll be asking about, and reassure him or her that you will be getting to each topic. While it might be difficult, it's important not to interrupt if they go off on a tangent. Let them talk; they might even reveal an answer to a question you hadn't yet asked, or they might open the door to questions you never thought to ask.

To begin, start by asking one question and recording the answer in this book. Be prepared that Grandpa might answer a question you had asked Grandma, or vice versa. This is rather common in grandparents. When it happens, rephrase the question by asking, "Grandma, how would you answer that in your own words?" Be polite, but make sure that you are getting the answers and the perspective from the right person. There are plenty of questions to ask each grandparent, plus you can change a question if you would prefer to ask it of the other grandparent.

As you begin to learn more about your grandparents, think about what a wonderful gift you are building for yourself. Consider the unique tendencies and habits that you have—you got most of them indirectly from your grandparents. Isn't it nice to have a record of the people who helped shape your parents, who then helped to shape you?

If you are not fortunate enough to have both of your grandparents still here with you, you can still capture many of these memories from just one of them. Ask your Grandma how grandpa would have answered the question. Even if neither grandparent is alive, you can still learn about them. It will take a little more effort, but the result will bring you joy for years to come. There are several ways you can go about gathering this information. We have three suggestions:

1. The next time there is a family gathering—it can be as big as Thanksgiving dinner or as simple as a summer outing—pull out this book. Tell your family that you want to get some information about your grandparents. You might start by asking which personality type seems to best identify them. Don't be surprised when you hear some differing opinions. Each of the relatives will have seen and known them for different periods. Settle in on the one type that best "fits your picture" of them. Read a question and then ask, "How would Grandma (or Grandpa) have answered that?" You will likely hear several responses to any one question; there might even be a few differences in the answers. That's okay; write them all down if you can.

2. Write out some of the questions on your own paper, and send them out to family members and friends who were close to your grandparents. Provide some explanation about this new project you are working on. Tell them you have a lot of questions you are trying to answer as if your grandma and grandpa

were answering them for you. Let these people know that there is not a time deadline, but you would appreciate their sending back anything they have within a month. As a courtesy, enclose a self-addressed stamped envelope in with your letter.

3. Buy extra copies of this book. Write up a cover letter telling everyone what you are doing. Then send two copies of the book along with your cover letter to family members and friends. Ask them to fill out as much as they can in one of the books and send it back to you. (Send them a prepaid envelope to make it easier.) The other book is for them to keep—they can use it to develop their own keepsake of your grandma and grandpa, or they could use it to begin their own journey to find out more about their own grandparents.

We send our best wishes to you as you begin your quest to develop a deeper knowledge of your family roots through your grandparents.

"Not All Grandparents Are the Same"

IT REALLY SHOULDN'T surprise you that not all grandparents are the same. We know that instinctively, yet most of us generalize that grandparents are, well, they are grandparents. You can probably even see this in your own grandparents—Grandpa on your mom's side is not the same as Grandpa on your dad's side of the family. Think of some of the elderly whom you know and picture them in "their role" as a grandmother or a grandfather. Is there something in their demeanor or hobbies they have that sets them apart from the others?

Not only is one set of grandparents different from another set, you also know that your grandma and your grandpa have different likes and dislikes. When you read the section "What Grandma enjoys to keep her busy," you will be finding many types that can apply to your grandma. The same thing is true as you go through the section "What do you think of first when you think of Grandpa?" Many of them apply to him. Just like there are millions of people who have a birthday on the same day as you, there are millions of grandmas and grandpas who share similar traits and activities.

Rather than focus on the similarities of the millions of grandparents out there, you have this book so you can document the things that make your grandma and your grandpa unique. As you read through the different activities that keep Grandma busy, you are going to find several of them that jump right out and say, "That's my grandma!" You might even say that all of them fit her. And as you are reading the grandpa traits, you will be thinking to yourself, "That one fits him, and that one fits him, and so does that one!" That is natural because grandparents—just like all people—are multidimensional. There are many activities they like to do, and there are many characteristics that describe who they are.

The relationships that we have with our grandparents are different from those we have with our parents. It is okay to think of more than one "Grandma activity" or "Grandpa trait" when someone asks about them.

Some of us have grandparents who are retired and are in their seventies or eighties—or even older. There are even those whose grandparents are still working and are many years away from their first Social Security check! Not all grandparents spend a lot of time in the rocking chair on the front porch; many of them have vibrant lives and active social calendars. As you read the sections and questions to follow, keep in mind that the activity or trait might fit your grandparent even if an age description seems out of place. Rewrite the text if it makes sense to have it be more like *your* grandma or grandpa.

The Importance of Learning More about Grandma and Grandpa

You might be wondering why it really matters to know what type best fits your grandma or grandpa. It's not critical for your relationship with them, but it gives you an edge as you start to learn more about them. And as you delve deeper into their thoughts and memories, you'll discover more about your parents, and even yourself. As much as you might not want to admit it, you are (or you will be) like your parents in many ways. They, in turn, developed many of the habits of their parents. But the reason you want to know more about your grandparents is not just to "see what you will be like many years from now"; the reason is so you can build and strengthen the relationship with people who have influenced your life.

At this point we are going to split into a "Grandma" section and a "Grandpa" section to keep it clear for you as you embark on this journey. When the questions begin to focus on Grandma and

Grandpa's life, their family history, and their values, there will be combined questions for them rather than one for Grandma and one for Grandpa.

What Grandma Enjoys to Keep Busy

Listed below are nine activities that many grandmothers enjoy. Are there more? Of course. But as you'll discover, it's not the actual activity that is important, but rather the ability to ask questions based on each type's preferred activities and hobbies. By asking targeted questions, you will be relating to her on a new level that will make her feel unique and special.

Begin by browsing through the list without trying to focus too hard on which is "the right activity" that describes Grandma. Put the book down for a couple minutes and close your eyes. Picture your grandma as you would see her if you arrived unannounced at her house. What is it that you would find her to be doing? It's not just what she is doing, but what are the activities that put a smile on her face? Now pick the book back up and reread through the list. If none jump out at you, do you see one particular activity that stands out a little more than the rest? Even if there are two or three that seem to be the right ones, that is okay. In fact, having more than one primary activity will give you more opportunities to ask Grandma some probing questions that will tell you a little more about her. We have included some questions in this book that are specific to each type so you can focus in on her life and the activities she really enjoys.

Active in her faith—This grandma feels a special bond to her faith and she finds true enjoyment in her participation. She might be seen doing work in the office, or she might be calling members who have not been feeling well. If there is a get-together, she is either the planner or one of the first ones there to set up the tables and help with the organizing. She volunteers not only because of her strong beliefs, but this is also a key way for her to maintain the friendship with those who share the same connection. You will know that this describes your grandma because of the friends who are there when you arrive, the telephone calls, or the ones who just stop by "for a chat." They will talk about an upcoming fundraiser or a mutual friend who needs some help. The conversation typically concludes with well wishes and that they will see each other on the weekend. They might talk about some of the specifics of their faith, but Grandma knows that not everyone is as comfortable talking about their faith as she is. If you ask her, she will talk with you about her beliefs, but she is not one to force her beliefs upon you or anyone else. She is a leader, maybe not in a specific role, but by the fact that she gets things done.

What makes you so strong in your faith?

What bonding do you feel with your friends when you are with them?

Do you see yourself as a role model for others who see you as a leader?

"Bucking" the system—This grandma was a rebel in "her day." If there was a cause to march for, or demonstrate against, Grandma was probably right there in the middle of it. She continues to buck the system today, although she now resorts to more subtle ways. She will write a letter to the editor of the local newspaper to comment on the latest city hall issue, or if there is a business that always gets away with "breaking the law." She is the one who will put a controversial sign in her yard, and she probably has a bumper sticker on her car to support an underprivileged group somewhere in the world. Her TV will not be tuned to a mainstream news program, and she really does not like the "talking heads," who she believes talk just so they can hear their own voice. When asked, she will take a petition around the neighborhood to ask for signatures. She will be the one at a local news conference who is holding a sign asking the question that the politicians won't answer—but the sign does get TV coverage. When you sit down for a quiet one-on-one conversation with this grandma, she will tell you that what she is doing is "nothing compared to what we used to do when I was younger and had more energy."

What results have you seen from taking a stand for what you believe is right and just?

Who are some of the friends you have made as you rallied for a certain cause?

What's the one outrageous thing you've done that, as you look back on it today, you can't believe that you actually did that?

Cleaning house—This grandma's house is always spotlessly clean. You wonder how she manages to keep it that way all the time. But then it makes sense because whenever you see her she is cleaning something. (Now you see why your parents were always on your case about having a clean room!) The wood floors are always shiny but not slippery. The windows are clear, even after a hard rain. When you ask her about it, she says that she likes to have a clean house so visitors feel comfortable when they are there. While Grandma's house is always clean, it is not the type of "clean" that makes you feel as if you cannot sit anywhere or touch anything. It is "grandma clean," not "glamorous magazine clean." One side benefit of having a grandma who likes cleaning is that she can give you many tips on what you can do to save time (and money) as you clean your room, your apartment, or your own house. If you ask her nicely, and not too often, she just might even come over to help you (as she shows you how).

Your house is always so clean. What is that you value about keeping things in order?

What was it that your Mom instilled in you to make sure your house is always clean and inviting for friends and family?

Is it hard for you to not say anything when you see other peoples' houses that are never picked up, or it doesn't look like they've used a dust rag in over a month? What are you thinking in those situations?

Cooking—Saying that this grandma loves to cook is a major understatement. The amazing thing is that she makes it seem so easy, and it is never a bother for her to prepare a meal for two or for twenty-two. If there is a special occasion or a need for a "potluck meal," Grandma will be the first one to volunteer. When she offers to bring a dessert for a dinner gathering, always accept her offer because not only do you know the dessert will be delicious, but this is also what she believes is the courteous way to accept an invitation. Never tell her, "No, thanks, Grandma. I already have ice cream." Not only is she comfortable cooking for family and friends, she is quite adept at making "in season" meals from the local foods and from her garden. She also can take a recipe and modify it to use the freshest fruit or the vegetables that were just picked. To really get on her good side, ask for meal suggestions, or even how to prepare a recipe. You are not trying to get her to do the work, you just want to pass on her knowledge—something she will gladly do.

How did you become such a good cook? Did you do a lot of the cooking when you were a youngster at home?

Are there any prized family recipes that you want to see us hand down and say that they came from Grandma or another relative?

Do you ever watch any of the cooking shows on TV? What do you like about them?

Crafting—This grandma has many crafts that she enjoys, so she might be knitting one time, and then doing some crochet another time. She makes seasonal items when she is crafting and you will see them around the house. Even though sewing is not her favorite activity, Grandma is the one to call when there is a play that needs costumes made—she is creative and can make them to meet a quick deadline. Not only is she a good seamstress, she can tell you what styles look good on you (hint: take Grandma clothes shopping with you; you will like her inputs better than your parents').

Have you ever belonged to a craft group? If so, did you attend more for the crafting or for the social interaction?

How does knitting or one of your other crafts help to relieve the stress from work and your other daily activities?

Do you always go by a pattern, or can you design it as you go?

Gardening—This grandma could go by the nickname "Grandma Green Thumb" because of her ability to make anything and every-thing grow just right. She looks forward to spring when she can plant her new crops, even if it's just a couple tomato plants, a squash, and some peppers. If she has more land, she will typically have it divided into little plots that allow her to manage her garden as well as keep it neatly organized. Grandma gardens for several reasons: she really likes to have fresh food; she does not want to be dependent on the big stores; she likes working outside in the fresh air, and she likes the independence that it gives her. When you visit Grandma, be prepared to accept whatever is currently growing in her garden. This means that you better learn to like everything she grows because she is going to give you some—and you CANNOT say "No" to her offer. She will occasionally forget to wear those nice gardening gloves that you gave her. The truth is that she likes having her hands in the soil because she can tell by its feel if it needs any additives or more water. Because Grandma spends so much weekend time gardening outside, you will have a hard time reaching her on the phone. She also uses this time as a break from her work schedule.

When and where did you learn so much about gardening?

What is your favorite fruit or vegetable? Was it one that you liked to eat as a youngster, or did you acquire the taste for it later?

Do you have a favorite recipe for items from your garden? Is it a recipe that has been in your family for a long time or is it a new one?

What is your favorite time of day for gardening? Why?

Reminisces about the "good old days"—Typically alone, she talks about previous times in her life because she likes to remember all those happy memories. She might display a few recent photos of her grandchildren, but all the other ones are old family photos. Because Grandma likes to "live in years gone by," her favorite television programs will be shows that are no longer running. There might be one current show that she watches, but the vast majority will be reruns. She identifies with the era in which these shows aired, but she will tell you that the main reason she watches them is that "there are no good, clean shows on TV anymore." When you visit with Grandma, you can pull her out from "looking backward" by talking about what you've been up to—this helps to bring her focus forward to current activities. When she brings up older situations or wants to talk about "Back when I was young," listen to her for a while—she is your grandma and she deserves your respect. When you can, find a way to transition that conversation into more current and positive discussions. She will go along with you; you just need to be gentle about it.

What can you tell me about when you and Grandpa were first married? Is there anything you will tell me that you never told your own children?

Who was your favorite movie star when you were my age?

Many teenagers have their own car today. When did you get your first car, and what was it like?

Researching and recording family history—Always busy working on family trees for her family and friends, this grandma feels like she's working on a history project, and in a way she really is. She is working to record the family history that most people think they "know," or are just too busy to work on themselves. When you ask Grandma about one of her aunts or uncles, she will pull out an old family Bible or another book and show you the family tree that was written there. She will uncover some surprises in the family history that are usually not talked about—unless you ask her at the right time. The person you always called "Uncle Fred" might not actually be your uncle at all. So why was he called "Uncle Fred"? Maybe that's a question you ask Grandma when it is just the two of you talking. While Grandma is mostly focused on family history, she can be a great resource whenever you need to do some research or find information. She knows how to ask the right questions, and she knows the right people to ask.

How did you get started working on family history? Was there someone further back in our family tree who got you curious?

What is the most interesting thing that you have found out about our family as you have done your research? How did you find it?

As you have researched other families, have you uncovered anything that you did not feel comfortable passing along to those people? What did you do?

Visiting with friends and family—This is definitely a social grandma. She loves to be with family and friends, and she's comfortable talking as well as listening. If you ever want to hear a really good story, just ask Grandma to tell you one. She can tell you stories about your parents that they will never tell you. She is a good friend to her neighbors, and she can be counted on to call on anyone who is not feeling well. She enjoys the communal benefits of being with other people and making them feel good. She does not always come straight home from work because she might be stopping to visit a friend. An ideal vacation for her would be to travel around the country to spend a few days with some friends. The local sights would not be as important to her as being able to spend time with people who mean so much to her. When it is time to have a special party for Grandma, make sure you have plenty of room for entertaining because you will have lots of her friends show up to help her celebrate.

Who are some of your closest friends? How long have you known them, and where did you meet them?

Where would be the ideal place for you to have a once-in-a-lifetime vacation with friends and family?

Have you been able to make really good friends with the people you work with?

Which one of your friends would be the first one to come over if you really needed their help?

What do you think of first when you think of Grandpa?

Listed below are nine traits that many grandfathers have. We are sure that you can name many more, but the point is for you to find one that reminds you of Grandpa when you think of him. The ones we have listed are traits that identify him and allow you to ask him some specific questions. As you begin to learn more about Grandpa, you will see that it is not the type that is important, but rather the ability to ask questions based on each type's preferred activities and hobbies.

Begin by browsing through the list without trying to focus too hard on which trait best describes your grandpa. Put the book down for a couple minutes and close your eyes. Picture your grandpa as if a famous artist had painted a large portrait of him to hang in your house. What does he look like; what is he thinking about; what is he doing? What is the one main thing that you think of when you are going to describe him to someone else? Now pick the book back up and reread through the list. Does one of them stand out more than the others? Even if there are two or three that seem to be the right ones, that is okay. In fact, identifying more than one key trait will give you more opportunities to ask Grandpa some probing questions that will tell you a little more about him. We have included some questions that are specific to each type so you can focus in on his life and the activities he really enjoys.

Loves spending time with you—This grandpa is always happy to see you. He can be busy working in his shop, watching a TV show, or coming home from work. But as soon as he sees you, it is as if you are the most important person in the world. He will drop everything he is doing to give you a big hug and to just look at you. It is no coincidence that you are also happy to see him. He makes you feel special, and he will let you do almost anything you want to do (like the time he let you drive his car even though you didn't have your driver's license). When he sees you, or when you are talking with him on the phone, he will ask you, "How is my favorite grandson (or granddaughter)?" Even if you have siblings and cousins, and you are fairly sure that he says the same thing to them, you still feel extremely special because he makes you feel that way. Because Grandpa makes you feel so special and he always has time for you, you really look forward to every trip to see him and every time that he comes to visit you. Who needs another birthday present when you can spend time with such a loving Grandpa?

You make me feel so loved. Did you feel as loved as I am when you were my age?

How do you find the time to make each of your grandchildren feel so special?

What did you like to do when you were a kid? What were your favorite games?

Active outdoors—This grandpa just can't wait for the next "season" to begin. He is counting the weeks until he is able to "head back out." He loves to hunt, to fish, to do anything that allows him to be outdoors. When you go fishing with Grandpa, he will show you the right way to attach your lure so it won't come off when a big fish grabs it. He can make the best campfire even if you didn't see very much wood lying around the area. He's a natural in the outdoors environment, and he loves to share that excitement and knowledge with anyone. A sure bet to have him sit down and watch a program with you is to see what is on the Discovery Channel. He can probably deliver a more interesting narration than the announcer who is doing the show. While the show is on, ask Grandpa about some of the things that he has done, especially if he says something like, "When I was there" or "I was in that situation once." Be careful, however, because once he starts talking, it may take a while until he stops to "catch his breath."

How did you get so interested in hunting, fishing, etc.?

Did you ever get lost in the woods? What did you do to find your way back to camp or the trailhead?

What has been your most exciting outdoors adventure? Do you still see any of your friends who were with you? Do you work with any of them?

Grilling outside—This grandpa can cook anything outside on the barbeque. Even when Grandma has the oven ready to bake the main course, Grandpa will come in and say, "I'll just throw it on outside—how much time do I have?" The amazing thing is that he can cook anything so it tastes great. One of the main reasons that he likes to cook outdoors is so he can talk with people while he grills. He also likes to just be outside, but his great enjoyment comes from cooking on the BBQ. If you are ever trying to think of something to get for Grandpa, take a look at his grilling equipment the next time you are at his house. He probably does not wear a chef's hat, but he would look good with one perched on his head. One of the real benefits of Grandpa's love of barbequing is that he will be the duty chef whenever you go camping. He might not be used to cooking over a wood fire, but he will not make any excuses—just great food!

How did you learn to be such a barbeque expert? Who taught you?

Did you ever forget that you had something on the barbeque and walk away from it? What happened? What did Grandma say?

What is the largest crowd that you have cooked for? What sort of challenges did that present?

Is there anything that you just cannot cook on the barbeque (or that you would prefer not to)? Why is that?

Fixes anything—This grandpa is extremely popular with all the neighbors because he can, and does, fix anything. Doing this, however, means he has a workshop and a workbench that are always full of tools, parts, and half-completed fix-it projects. His weekends are usually busy while he works on a few neighborly projects. Grandpa is a tinkerer, and while some of his fix-it projects will work, they might not look "pretty." His concern is to get something working, not necessarily to get it working in the same way it originally did. Because he is so handy, there will always be neighbors stopping by to see if Grandpa "could just take a quick look" at whatever they have that is broken. He never wants to be paid for anything, even for the parts, because "I do this for fun—it's not work to me." He will accept a homemade pie if anyone really insists that he be paid. The downside to Grandpa's ability to fix anything is that he will tell you that you are wasting money if you call a repair service to come out to fix anything. You would love to let Grandpa fix it, but your timetable might not match with his for actually getting it fixed. You may have to get creative with your excuses when he asks why you didn't call him first.

How did you learn to be so handy?

Have you ever had any surprises when you were fixing something? Did you ever find any animals or insects hiding inside the item you were to fix? What did you do?

Did you ever "fix" anything that Grandma didn't want you to touch? Why didn't she want you to work on it? What did she say?

What has been the hardest thing for you to fix? What do you really like to work on?

Makes anything—This grandpa is like the "Mr. Fix-It Grandpa" except that he also can take a block of wood and make a whistle out of it, or turn it into a base for a new lamp. He is handy with all kinds of tools, and he will usually send you a handmade gift rather than a purchased one. When you go to a store with Grandpa, he will say things like, "I could make that for less than a third of what they want for it." And he probably could—although it might not have the same finished look to it. Plan to be busy when you visit Grandpa because he always has a few projects underway at various stages of completion. He cannot wait to get home from work, or for the weekend to start, so he can get back to his projects. Even when you go on a trip with Grandpa, he will be talking about some of his projects or getting ideas for new ones. Take some mental notes on the process he uses to store this information, whether on note pads or in his head. He might use the computer to find old parts to fix a model train, but the real work is done in his head and on scratch paper.

How did you get so handy? Did you take some shop classes in school, or did you just learn it by practice?

Have you ever made anything that Grandma really wanted to buy instead? Does she still have it, or did it "accidentally" fall off and get broken?

What have you made that gave you the greatest feeling of accomplishment?

What projects have you had to start over? What happened?

Do you have any funny stories about something you were working on?

Collecting—This grandpa is a collector junky. Whether he likes model trains, history books, soda cans, or art work, he is extremely dedicated to his collecting. He would probably collect antique cars if he had a garage big enough to house them. He can tell you every-thing about his particular hobby and he knows the details of every item in his collection. He is handy at the computer because he is always looking online for another item to add, and he probably has his collection catalogued on the computer. A really interesting note is that his hobby most likely has nothing to do with what he does for work (or did, if he is now retired). He views collecting as a diversion from work, so this is really fun to him. If you show interest in Grand-pa's collection, you will earn immediate entrance to his "A list."

How did you get started collecting? What was the first item you got? Do you still have it?

Which one is your favorite? What is so special about it?

Who are some of the people you have met because of your collection?

Reading—This grandpa is well-read, not only in the clas-sics, but also in current events and popular trade novels. No mat-ter where he goes, he has something with him to read—a book, a magazine, or a newspaper article. He views life as one constant education process, and that is how he looks at reading—he is giving his mind a continual education. A side benefit of his reading is that Grandpa has a good command of vocabulary and he is not afraid to get involved in intellectual discussions or debates. Despite his knowledge, he is not a "show off," and he will not put on airs that he knows more than others. He remains humble; he just likes to read. If you ever want to have some private time with Grandpa, just ask him if he would like to go to the bookstore with you. A bookstore to Grandpa is like a candy store to most kids. He will stroll through the aisles looking at all types of books. There might be a genre or two that he is extremely interested in, but he also likes to read books that are somewhat unusual or steeped in pop culture. The only downside to Grandpa's love of reading is that he might not be interested in watching drag racing or motocross, but he just might surprise you if you invite him. A real plus for you is that you'll always know he'll thoroughly enjoy anything related to books.

Do you have a favorite author? Who is it, and why?

If you were stranded on an island, what would be the five books that you would want to have with you? What is so special about each one of them?

When did you first realize that you had this love of books? What brought it on?

What book have you read more times than any other? How many times? Why?

Tells wonderful stories—This grandpa is popular wherever he goes because he is able to entertain everyone with his exciting stories. He has told you many stories about when he was young, about when he was in the war—the "Big One"—and even some stories about your parents (ones they have never told you). Even though most of his stories are personal and true, he is also able to "spin a good yarn" when he is with some of his friends. While it's always fun to visit with Grandpa, the downside is that he is popular, so you can't expect to be the center of attention when he is there. A natural phenomenon with this type of grandpa is that Grandma will typically be quiet—this is because he has always done most of the "talking," and so she has adapted by staying quiet. You will have to either pull her aside to talk or really ask her to open up. It's not something she is used to, but she can do it. Something that might really surprise you is how popular Grandpa can be with people in your own generation. They will love to be entertained by him, and he will be in his own element telling stories and making people laugh.

When did you realize that you have a gift for talking, telling stories, and keeping people entertained?

Did you ever get in trouble when you are a youngster because of your talking? What would your teachers say to you?

What is your favorite story to tell? Why?

Travels—This grandpa is a born wanderer. He likes his home, but he really loves being out on the road seeing new things and visiting old friends. Grandpa likes to visit some exotic foreign places, but he is just as happy driving around from one city or state to the next. He does not keep a list of which states he has been in (although he knows them by heart), and he does not feel that he has to collect a decal or refrigerator magnet from all fifty of the United States. Even though he does like to visit a few other countries, he will tell you that he saw enough of Europe or Asia when he was in the military. That is just his way of saying that he likes places closer to home. Because he does like to travel, Grandpa is someone you can talk with when you are considering a vacation of your own. Ask him about places you've considered visiting, and see what he has to say about them. Ask him a direct question, "Would you recommend that I go there?" He will give you a comfortable answer, so you will have to press him a little harder if you don't think that he is being entirely open with you. A fun trip would be to know when he is going to be somewhere and then you just "show up" and surprise him. That can be a great time for both of you.

What is your favorite place to visit? Why? How many times have you been there?

Is there someplace you have not been but want to get there "some day"?

Who are some special friends you have met when you were traveling? Do you still keep in touch with them?

What is your favorite way to travel? Plane, car, train, boat? Why? Is there one you don't want to do?

Why It's Important to Connect with Your Grandma and Grandpa

- Many of us have not been fortunate enough to spend lots of time with our grandma and grandpa. As you went through the previous sections and tried to figure out "what Grandma enjoys to keep her busy" and "what you think of first when you think of Grandpa," you were embarking on the first steps of a journey to capture precious memories that you will have forever.

- As you begin to know more about these special people, you will also now have more insight into what they might really like the next time you want to get something for them. Perhaps you are on a trip to some other country that you have heard them talk about; is there a small item you can find that now has special meaning for them? It's a gift they're guaranteed to like, not only because it is from you, but also because it ties in with one of their favorite activities.

As we mentioned earlier, one of the key advantages of knowing more about your grandparents is that they are the ones who molded your parents. As you learn more about Grandma and Grandpa, you will begin to learn more about why your parents are they way they are, or why they insist that you do something a particular way. You will also have an inside look at who your parents will become as they get older, and how they might act as grandparents to your own children one day.

Learning more about your grandparents is important because it will help you better understand your family history. Even if you have to talk with other people to find out about them, you are capturing a piece of your own heritage that will be very special to you some day. Gather as much information as possible while you can. The worst regret we can have is to someday say, "I wish I had talked with my grandparents so I could have learned more about them." Do it now; do it today; do it so you have no regrets tomorrow.

Part 2
Questions
to Ask Your
Grandma and Grandpa

Now that you know so much about Grandma and Grandpa, you will be able to approach the following questions with more ease and comfort. Your parents might have already told you some things about them, but you will be surprised how much more you learn once you start to talk with them about their childhood, dreams, and goals.

While the question pages may resemble a notebook to be filled out, the value comes from what you learn while talking with your grandparents. This is not a notebook to fill out just so it is finished once you have written something on every page. There are no grades, and no one is going to evaluate what you have done (or not done) when you are finished. The only one who will know how well you did is you. What you are doing is gathering information to preserve your grandparents' legacies today so you have no regrets tomorrow. We don't know how much time we will have with our grandma and grandpa, so it is imperative that we gather and record as much as we can now—while we can. If this indicates a sense of urgency, then you have gotten the message. Don't wait to talk with them—get started immediately!

In case you need a reminder on how to ask the questions, turn to the earlier section "How to Use This Book." Some of the questions to follow might be just for Grandma or just for Grandpa, and those will either be obvious to you, or you might only want to ask one of them. For the questions that you want to ask each of them, write both of their answers in the space, expanding into the margins if you have to.

On Grandma and Grandpa's Lives

"All my life through, the new sights of Nature made me rejoice like a child."
Marie Curie

The questions in this section offer a glimpse into what Grandma and Grandpa remember as some of the highlights of their child-hoods and lives. Consider this the ideal place to begin a conversation, offering them a listening ear and an interested mind. They can be a wealth of stories and insights, and the more you learn, the more you'll remember about them. Plus, Grandma and Grandpa will appreciate and enjoy the opportunity to share those special moments from their past and what's especially meaningful to them.

As they reflect on childhood memories, have them move back in time to when they were young. Find out what was important to them—and be prepared for different answers. Unless they grew up in the same area, they undoubtedly had very different childhood experiences.

Like a puzzle, there will be so many aspects of their lives that will overlap. As they answer a question, keep them focused on that specific topic. There will be plenty of questions you will ask that relate to a wide scope of themes as you continue.

Begin by sharing with Grandma and Grandpa that these questions are an overview of their lives, how they have lived it, and the highlights. Stay centered on each question, asking them to share something specific as you progress. For example, if Grandpa starts talking about when he sneaked out of school to go fishing, there is probably more to find out than just that part. Did he go with anyone else? Did they get caught? What was their punishment? Which one was worse—the teacher's punishment or the parents'? Did he ever do it again?

Pay special attention to their expressions as they are talking with you about memories that are such an integral part of who they are, and who you are. If you look very carefully, you will see a slight smile come to Grandma's face as she reminisces about those happy times from so many years ago. Capture the expressions she is using—not just the words, but the hand motions, the way she lifts her head to the left and looks into space where all of those dear images are stored. Seal into your own memory bank the calm look on her face; that image could turn out to be one of your dearest memories of her. Grandpa's expressions are also important to capture. Notice how similar they are in some respects, and how different they are in others.

What are some of your earliest memories about your birthplace and growing up?

_____

_____

_____

_____

_____

_____

_____

_____

_____

_____

_____

_____

_____

Who were some of your childhood friends and what special memories do you recall about the times you shared with them?

_____

_____

_____

_____

_____

_____

_____

_____

_____

_____

_____

_____

_____

Did you and your friends have a favorite place to play? Can you describe it and some of the things you would do there?

_____

_____

_____

_____

_____

_____

_____

_____

_____

_____

_____

_____

Grandma, how did others describe you when you were a young girl?

_____

_____

_____

_____

_____

_____

_____

_____

_____

_____

_____

_____

_____

Grandpa, how did others describe you when you were a young boy?

_____

_____

_____

_____

_____

_____

_____

_____

_____

_____

_____

_____

_____

What was it like going to school? Did you go to a large school, or was it small? Do you remember any particular teachers?

_____

_____

_____

_____

_____

_____

_____

_____

_____

_____

_____

_____

_____

What activities did you do after school? What kinds of jobs were available for students back then—either in high school or after high school?

_____

_____

_____

_____

_____

_____

_____

_____

_____

_____

_____

_____

_____

When did you first learn to drive? Who taught you how to drive? What was your first car?

_____

_____

_____

_____

_____

_____

_____

_____

_____

_____

_____

_____

_____

Can you recall how much a loaf of bread cost when you were a teenager? How much was a gallon of gas when you first started to drive?

_ _

_ _

_ _

_ _

_ _

_ _

_ _

_ _

_ _

_ _

_ _

_ _

_ _

What accomplishments in your life are you proudest of?

_____

_____

_____

_____

_____

_____

_____

_____

_____

_____

_____

_____

_____

Is there anything you have done in your life that you regret?

_ _

_ _

_ _

_ _

_ _

_ _

_ _

_ _

_ _

_ _

_ _

_ _

_ _

_ _

How old were you when you got your first television? What was your favorite show?

_____

_____

_____

_____

_____

_____

_____

_____

_____

_____

_____

_____

_____

" On Our Family History "

> *"Even as the cell is the unit of the organic body, so the family is the unit of society."*
>
> Ruth Nanda Anshen

Grandma and Grandpa's family history helped shape them into the people they became. That same history is what formed your parents into who they are. The following questions are very important, for they pay a loving tribute to your grandparents' life, including their parents and family. Their family history also impacts yours and your children's lives, so pay attention to the little details you learn along the way.

This section contains questions you can ask Grandma and Grandpa about their families and childhood activities. This also gives you a chance to gain more understanding of what it was like "back then," and what events shaped their lives. We are all a product of our upbringing, and this section allows that history to come alive and present itself to you. You might not like everything you hear or read, but all of it is a part of the makeup of who your parents are and who you are.

When you hear or read something about your family history that you did not already know, ask a probing question to learn even more and get beyond the superficial answer. For example, if your Grandpa says that he had to leave school after the eighth grade to work to support the family, find out if that is why your own parents feel so strongly about education. When Grandma talks about helping her own mother prepare the meals, probe further to find out more about some of her recipes and her penchant for "fresh ingredients."

When you start to write down the information you want to pass along to your children, this section on your grandparents' family history will be very important. This is where your children will find out about the relatives they will probably never meet. Even if you have not had much interaction with your grandparents, they provided the framework for who you and your children are. This section can really be fun because you are able to learn so much more about other members of the family tree—those aunts and uncles whom you would see occasionally but never spent much time with. These are the people who are the very core of your family roots.

Depending on the family dynamics in your grandparents' lives, this section might be a little touchy. You probably already know that, however, and so it will not be a surprise to you. If this is the case, we suggest that you save this section for after you have already talked with them on several other sections. By beginning with the "easier" sections, you will have been able to establish a rapport that becomes more conversational rather than like an interview. Once you have developed that bond and you can ask almost anything—then you can come back to this section.

Is there anything you wish you could have asked your parents, but never got around to?

_____

_____

_____

_____

_____

_____

_____

_____

_____

_____

_____

_____

_____

What would you like future generations to know about you, my parents, and our family history?

_____

_____

_____

_____

_____

_____

_____

_____

_____

_____

_____

_____

_____

What was the best advice your Mom or Dad gave you when you were younger that has always stayed on your mind?

_ _

_ _

_ _

_ _

_ _

_ _

_ _

_ _

_ _

_ _

_ _

_ _

_ _

Can you share what you loved most about your father? What is one story about him that you would want passed to the next generations?

_____

_____

_____

_____

_____

_____

_____

_____

_____

_____

_____

_____

_____

Can you share what you loved most about your mother? What is one special memory of her that made you feel special?

_____

_____

_____

_____

_____

_____

_____

_____

_____

_____

_____

_____

_____

Can you share any special traditions, gatherings or family get-togethers that you especially remember?

_ _

_ _

_ _

_ _

_ _

_ _

_ _

_ _

_ _

_ _

_ _

_ _

_ _

How did you get along with your brothers and sisters? What special stories do you remember about them? If you are an only child, were there special friends who seemed like a brother or a sister to you?

_____

_____

_____

_____

_____

_____

_____

_____

_____

_____

_____

_____

_____

What family member did you most look up to and want to be like?

_____

_____

_____

_____

_____

_____

_____

_____

_____

_____

_____

_____

_____

What do you think made our family special that you hope is carried on by the next generations?

_____

_____

_____

_____

_____

_____

_____

_____

_____

_____

_____

_____

_____

What are some of the special family books or other heirlooms that you want kept in the family?

_____

_____

_____

_____

_____

_____

_____

_____

_____

_____

_____

_____

_____

On Grandma and Grandpa's Values

"All life demands struggle. Those who have everything given to them become lazy, selfish, and insensitive to the real values of life. The very striving and hard work that we so constantly try to avoid is the major building block in the person we are today."

Pope Paul VI

This section focuses on the values that are important to Grandma and Grandpa. These are the beliefs that they live their lives by and what challenged our parents to be the best people they could be. As you ask each of them the principles that they care most about, consider your own values. Did you learn them from your parents? Did they encourage you to live your life by these guiding thoughts and ideals? Are you following along the path that you know you should? It's not easy to do, but an honest, open reflection on what your grandparents believed might help you when you face times that require some serious soul searching.

Many people automatically connect having values to being "religious." There certainly can be a connection there, but *everyone* can have values in their life; and we know that not everyone is religious. Or it might be that their "religion" is not one that we understand. That is okay. Our values are the core of what we are and who we are. Have you ever been in a situation where you could have "gotten away with something," but you chose the honorable way? Why did you make the right choice? Were you afraid that someone might see you and you'd feel guilty? Or did you do the right thing primarily because it was the right thing to do? If you chose the latter as the reason, then you have the right values. Think about this question from the previous paragraph—Did you learn your values from your parents? And where did they learn them? From Grandma and Grandpa?

A valid question that you might want to ask us is this: "But what if my grandparents' values are *not* the ones that I really want to mirror?" We do not want to do any preaching in this book about moral judgments or what is right and what is wrong. You're a grownup, and you can make those choices for yourself. Just remember that it is a very strong person who can acknowledge family heritage that is not the most ideal and shouldn't be continued. Second, always remember that your grandparents grew up in a vastly different environment and they may have been in situations where they did some things they did not *want* to do, but felt that they *had* to do. Please give them the benefit of the doubt and try to look for the positive side.

What one or two things would you want me to be certain of, to know, or to understand, as I go through life?

_____

_____

_____

_____

_____

_____

_____

_____

_____

_____

_____

_____

_____

Are you afraid of dying? What is it that you fear most? What will you miss the most?

_____

_____

_____

_____

_____

_____

_____

_____

_____

_____

_____

_____

_____

Do you feel that people of my generation have different values and morals than you had when you were my age? If so, why do you think that is?

_____

_____

_____

_____

_____

_____

_____

_____

_____

_____

_____

_____

_____

How did you impress the "right values" to your children? Have you seen them hold on to those values as they themselves became parents?

_____

_____

_____

_____

_____

_____

_____

_____

_____

_____

_____

_____

_____

Has your faith ever been tested? How did you handle it? What advice do you have for me?

_____

_____

_____

_____

_____

_____

_____

_____

_____

_____

_____

_____

How do you handle disappointment? What example can you give me so that I can be better prepared when I have to face it?

_____

_____

_____

_____

_____

_____

_____

_____

_____

_____

_____

_____

What do you do if you do not get something that you feel you deserve or have earned?

_____

_____

_____

_____

_____

_____

_____

_____

_____

_____

_____

_____

Can you share a motto you have lived your life by, or a good deed you have performed that gave you the greatest satisfaction? What was your inspiration at the time?

_____

_____

_____

_____

_____

_____

_____

_____

_____

_____

_____

_____

_____

What do you value most when it comes to friends, and what type of a friend are you to others?

_____

_____

_____

_____

_____

_____

_____

_____

_____

_____

_____

_____

_____

If you could change one thing about yourself, what would it be? What insight can you share about why you would want to make that change?

_____

_____

_____

_____

_____

_____

_____

_____

_____

_____

_____

_____

_____

What changes have you seen in people in general about caring for others?

_____

_____

_____

_____

_____

_____

_____

_____

_____

_____

_____

_____

_____

On Marriage and Relationships

"One should believe in marriage as in the immortality of the soul."

Honoré de Balzac

The topic of love, marriage, and relationships is certainly an important one. Approach these questions with care. While most grandparents willingly address these topics freely, others are more reserved to address their relationships. This might be an area where you have to tread lightly. If it's possible, this could be a fun area to include your own parents because they have most likely not asked these questions of their parents before.

Consider what's important in this section for you to accomplish. What do you really want to know? What might help you later in life as you deal with relationship issues or otherwise? Perhaps you want to better understand Grandma and Grandpa's feelings and these questions will help you see how they address personal relationships and what was passed on to your parents.

We know that some of you will have grandparents who are divorced or separated for other reasons. That does not mean that you should not ask these questions. You may have to approach them in a slightly different manner, but it is still very important to know their feelings. After you have worked through several of the "easier" sections, one way to approach this one is to say something like "We are now coming to some questions that might seem a bit awkward given the circumstances. But I know that you must have cared a lot about Grandpa (or Grandma, as appropriate) when you two were married. Those are the feelings that I want to know about. Those are the memories that I hope you can share with me." You are asking them to address some issues that are probably very difficult, especially if it has been a long time since the separation. Don't press the issue if they are not ready to answer these questions right now. You can always come back to them later— they know you will be coming back to them eventually. Grandma or Grandpa might even bring up the subject on his or her own. Once that happens, you will be given a wealth of information.

In addition to marriage, do your Grandma and Grandpa have other relationships that have been formed over the years? Are there people from work, or around the neighborhood, that they seem to enjoy spending time with? Do they like to visit certain people when they travel? Or are there certain friends who always come to visit them? As you find out more about these other people in their life, you will learn more about how they value relationships and why they are important. You will also gain more insight into the reasons behind your family and some of the dynamics that took place over many years.

Why do you think marriages don't last as long as they used to?

_____

_____

_____

_____

_____

_____

_____

_____

_____

_____

_____

_____

_____

_____

Did you give any special advice to your children when they were getting married? Did they listen to you?

_____

_____

_____

_____

_____

_____

_____

_____

_____

_____

_____

_____

_____

How did you first meet? What were your first thoughts? Was it love at first sight? What can you share about your first date?

_____

_____

_____

_____

_____

_____

_____

_____

_____

_____

_____

_____

_____

What is it about Grandma that makes you love her so much?

_____

_____

_____

_____

_____

_____

_____

_____

_____

_____

_____

_____

_____

What is it about Grandpa that makes you love him so much?

_____

_____

_____

_____

_____

_____

_____

_____

_____

_____

_____

_____

_____

When did you know that you wanted to get married? Do you remember the proposal? Was it serious or funny?

_____

_____

_____

_____

_____

_____

_____

_____

_____

_____

_____

_____

_____

What do you wish you knew "then," that you know now about relationships in life and in love?

Aside from family, who are some of the people in your life that you consider your "best friends"? What makes them so special, and what makes your relationship with them so special?

_____

_____

_____

_____

_____

_____

_____

_____

_____

_____

_____

_____

_____

On Grandma and Grandpa's Dreams and Goals

"Dream the impossible because dreams do come true."

Elijah Wood

More than anyone else, our grandparents hope for the future to be bright, happy, and prosperous because most of them had to work really hard to provide for their families. The future of their loved ones is so important to them. Search for what lessons they have learned in their lives, and encourage a conversation that will offer you insight into Grandma and Grandpa's past dreams and goals. You may even learn how they overcame adversity, rose to the occasion during difficult times, and obtained success while accomplishing what they had always hoped for.

As they answer these questions, try to dig deeper for more information. How were they feeling at the time? Did they know they were going to be successful, or did many people doubt them along the way? Who was giving them the encouragement they needed? What might have been the consequences if they had not succeeded? Even though there is a difference in age of forty to sixty years, these follow-on questions might give you additional insight that you can use when you are addressing similar situations. Share with them your own hopes and dreams because your success also is very important to them. They might even be willing to offer you some guidance on how they would handle the situations you are facing.

Your grandparents' generation was brought up with different goals than most of us have today—many of them came through very hard times when education typically took a back seat to making sure that the family had a roof over its head and food on the table. So it is not unusual if some of their goals might seem "simple" to you. Do not discount the fact that a primary motivator in their lives might have been to see their children go to college. What might now seem like a given to you could have been a stretch for them, and even for your parents. Your generation "has more" than Grandma and Grandpa's generation, so don't rush to judge them based on goals that you think are set too low. Remember that one of their primary concerns was "survival"—simple by most standards today, but that was the most important thing to them. Let them know how much you appreciate the sacrifices they made.

Once again, if there is any section where you do not want to be judgmental, this is it. If Grandma and Grandpa's dreams and goals sound mundane to you, try to put yourself in their position when they were your age—did they have any luxuries that you now consider necessities? Were they living at home while going to school, or were they working two jobs while still going to school? If you want to feel humble, put yourself in their shoes and see how you would survive.

When you were young, did you have any particular job or career that you envisioned yourself doing when you grew up? What attracted you to that?

_____

_____

_____

_____

_____

_____

_____

_____

_____

_____

_____

_____

_____

What is your greatest accomplishment in life? What would have been your answer ten years ago? Twenty years ago?

_____

_____

_____

_____

_____

_____

_____

_____

_____

_____

_____

_____

_____

What is one dream you have not made come true yet, but you hope one day to make happen?

_____

_____

_____

_____

_____

_____

_____

_____

_____

_____

_____

_____

_____

What are some "life lessons" that you impressed upon your children?

_____

_____

_____

_____

_____

_____

_____

_____

_____

_____

_____

_____

_____

_____

Do you think your children set their life goals too low? What else would you have liked to see them set out to accomplish?

_____

_____

_____

_____

_____

_____

_____

_____

_____

_____

_____

_____

_____

Can you share a time that you were disappointed because one of your goals or dreams did not come true, but you rose above it? How did you go about resetting your goal or your dream?

_____

_____

_____

_____

_____

_____

_____

_____

_____

_____

_____

_____

_____

Do you have any regrets in life that you wished you had done something differently? Is it too late to do it now?

_____

_____

_____

_____

_____

_____

_____

_____

_____

_____

_____

_____

_____

What goals do you think you might have if you were my age today? How different are they from those same goals when you were my age? What makes them different?

_____

_____

_____

_____

_____

_____

_____

_____

_____

_____

_____

_____

_____

_____

On Parenting, Children, and Being a Grandparent

"Children are not casual guests in our home. They have been loaned to us temporarily for the purpose of loving them and instilling a foundation of values on which their future lives will be built."

James Dobson

Being a parent is a full-time job. Your grandparents have already lived that job and now they have earned the right to sit back and observe. Most grandparents relish being a grandparent—it gives them certain privileges that they did not have when their primary role was raising a family. From supporting a family to raising children, a parent's responsibilities are often the core of their existence. This selection of questions focuses on the type of parent your grandparents were and how they viewed raising a family. It's a wonderful opportunity to let Grandma and Grandpa know that what they did as a parent helped mold you into the person you are today.

Once you become a parent, you also appreciate your own parents more than ever. It's a huge job and one of the most rewarding of life. The questions in this section will help you learn a great deal about life when you were born. Those little details can fade over time; from the day you were born to how your parents selected your name. This is an especially wonderful chapter since it's your heritage as well that Grandma and Grandpa will address. As they talk about you when you were very young and they would visit, they might get a little off-track in conversation—allow them that freedom. In fact, you can probably use these side conversations to find out even more about them. Even if there are not specific questions in this book along the lines that you are trying to get answered, this allows your grandparents more freedom to talk about things that could bring back wonderful memories for them.

If you are already a parent, then this chapter will have an extra special meaning. Ask some questions that will help you be the best parent you can be. Think about your own parenting style—what have you learned you are passing down to your children? What type of a grandparent would you like to be (someday)?

Use this section as a catalyst to gain clarity about what matters most to you and then consider how it affects your own children. This is a wonderful way to explore what kind of job you are doing as a parent and how you can incorporate your grandparents' wisdom and insights into your own parenting. If you uncover some family characteristics that you do not want to pass on to your children, keep that to yourself. This is another area where it might be easy to judge your parents (or your grandparents) in the way you were brought up—please don't. See what learnings you can take from those experiences and make the necessary adjustments in your own role as a parent.

Do you know the origins of your names? Were they family names that were passed on to you?

_____

_____

_____

_____

_____

_____

_____

_____

_____

_____

_____

_____

_____

What were your first thoughts when you heard my name? Did it surprise you? Is it spelled differently from how you would have spelled it?

_____

_____

_____

_____

_____

_____

_____

_____

_____

_____

_____

_____

_____

What family names did you want to see passed on? Are there names now that you would like to see used in the family?

_____

_____

_____

_____

_____

_____

_____

_____

_____

_____

_____

_____

_____

How soon after I was born did you first see me? Did you live nearby or did you have far to travel?

_____

_____

_____

_____

_____

_____

_____

_____

_____

_____

_____

_____

_____

What is one thing I have done that has made you proud of me?

_____

_____

_____

_____

_____

_____

_____

_____

_____

_____

_____

_____

What are some things your children did that made you proud of them? Did you ever tell them how proud that made you feel?

_____

_____

_____

_____

_____

_____

_____

_____

_____

_____

_____

_____

_____

How do you manage to unconditionally love your children, "no matter what"?

_____

_____

_____

_____

_____

_____

_____

_____

_____

_____

_____

_____

_____

If you were to give me one piece of advice based on what you have learned as a parent and as a grandparent that I should know and pass down to my children, what would it be?

_____

_____

_____

_____

_____

_____

_____

_____

_____

_____

_____

_____

_____

Do you think it was harder to raise children when my parents were young than it is today? What were some of the things you had to do then that are taken for granted today when raising a child?

_____

_____

_____

_____

_____

_____

_____

_____

_____

_____

_____

_____

_____

What are some things that my parents did while raising me that were different from the way that you raised Mom (or Dad)?

_____

_____

_____

_____

_____

_____

_____

_____

_____

_____

_____

_____

_____

How different is it being a grandparent than it was being a parent?

_____

_____

_____

_____

_____

_____

_____

_____

_____

_____

_____

_____

_____

On Grandma and Grandpa's Legacies

"The legacy we leave is not just in our possessions, but in the quality of our lives."

Billy Graham

This section contains questions that you can ask Grandma and Grandpa about what they want people to remember about them. When you think about your grandparents, it is important to know their thoughts, their feelings, their likes, their dislikes—all the things that make them unique and that they want people to never forget. You may even think you already know some of this, but take the time to let them tell you in their own words. After all, it is their legacy that you want to preserve. You can always talk with your parents to add just a little more than what your grandparents tell you—they were probably slightly modest in the initial answers they gave you.

None of us lives forever, but that does not mean that this section has to focus on our mortality. As you are asking these questions—try to focus on the things that truly reflect the essence of Grandma and Grandpa. As you look at a question, go beyond the simple one- or two-sentence answer. Expand on the answer with an example of something they did that made it very memorable—for them, for your parents, or for you. If your Grandpa wants to be known for being able to make almost anything out of a block of wood, take it an extra step and find out if there were ever any times when something funny happened as he was working on a project. Or perhaps he was just about done, and the saw slipped and cut it in half—and he had to start all over. Try to find that extra dimension in the answers that is not always offered out right away. Those are the stories that are fun to pass along. Was company coming over and Grandma making her special pie when she mixed up the amounts of baking powder and flour to use? The pie was a disaster but they all had a good laugh—except Grandma at the time!

Keep these thoughts in mind as you are talking with them about this section. You may have other thoughts, and that's okay. We just want to offer these as a guiding path in case you need one.

This section is devoted to helping Grandma and Grandpa craft the future. From what they want you to remember, to the words they hope you'll hear. Honor their lives by celebrating what they care about, believe in, and more. Let Grandma's legacy and Grandpa's legacy be based on love and instill upon your heart their words of wisdom and the insights into their lives. This is the time to make sure that you have everything you need to preserve their legacies today so you have no regrets tomorrow.

What is the main thing you want family members to know before you die?

_____

_____

_____

_____

_____

_____

_____

_____

_____

_____

_____

_____

_____

How do you want to be remembered?

_____

_____

_____

_____

_____

_____

_____

_____

_____

_____

_____

_____

_____

One day, when I am describing you to future generations, what would you want me to share about you?

_____

_____

_____

_____

_____

_____

_____

_____

_____

_____

_____

_____

_____

How can I show people that I have truly "learned" life's lessons from you?

_____

_____

_____

_____

_____

_____

_____

_____

_____

_____

_____

_____

What pictures of you should I hold most dear? What memories do they bring to you?

_____

_____

_____

_____

_____

_____

_____

_____

_____

_____

_____

_____

_____

What are some family memories that you want shared with anyone who asks about you?

_____

_____

_____

_____

_____

_____

_____

_____

_____

_____

_____

_____

_____

What are some key words that you want me to always remember? What special thoughts and feelings do they evoke for you?

_____

_____

_____

_____

_____

_____

_____

_____

_____

_____

_____

_____

_____

_____

"Who Knows Grandma and Grandpa Best?"

This section is especially important if you want to learn about Grandma and Grandpa through the eyes of others. This is very helpful if your grandparents are modest, won't say much, or perhaps are now deceased. Consider for a moment the amount of time your grandparents have spent with friends, other family members, and even coworkers. This is your chance to ask for their favorite memories of time spent with your grandparents and their feelings about them to preserve memories that perhaps would be long forgotten. While your parents might not view your grandparents in the same light as others would, it is valuable to talk with them just so that you have one more angle from which to view Grandma and Grandpa.

For those whose grandparent or grandparents are no longer with them, you will actually be doing a favor for those whom you contact. They will feel special because you have taken the time to ask them about your grandparents. There will be some tears shed, of course, as they tell you why they were so special. Think of those tears, and the ones you shed, as being the glue that ties all those special memories together.

There is less space for each of these questions, but you can photocopy these pages to ask more than two people the questions. There is even a little extra space in case you think of your own questions, or if one of the people you ask wants to give you even more information.

When did you meet my Grandma and how?

_____

_____

_____

_____

_____

_____

_____

_____

_____

_____

_____

_____

When did you meet my Grandpa and how?

_____

_____

_____

_____

_____

_____

_____

_____

_____

_____

_____

_____

_____

What are some of the most special memories you have of my grandparents?

_____

_____

_____

_____

_____

_____

_____

_____

_____

_____

_____

_____

Is there anything they taught you that inspired you and you recall to this day?

_____

_____

_____

_____

_____

_____

_____

_____

_____

_____

_____

_____

_____

Was there a time when my Grandma or Grandpa helped you in any way? How well did you know her or him, and how did it change your relationship?

_____

_____

_____

_____

_____

_____

_____

_____

_____

_____

_____

_____

If you were to describe your favorite things about my grandparents, what would they be?

_____

_____

_____

_____

_____

_____

_____

_____

_____

_____

_____

_____

_____

[to your own parent(s)] What are one or two things that Grandma and Grandpa instilled in you that you felt were extremely important?

_____

_____

_____

_____

_____

_____

_____

_____

_____

_____

_____

_____

When did you meet my Grandma and how?

_____

_____

_____

_____

_____

_____

_____

_____

_____

_____

_____

_____

_____

When did you meet my Grandpa and how?

_____

_____

_____

_____

_____

_____

_____

_____

_____

_____

_____

_____

_____

What are some of the most special memories you have of my grandparents?

_____

_____

_____

_____

_____

_____

_____

_____

_____

_____

_____

_____

_____

Is there anything they taught you that inspired you and you recall to this day?

_____

_____

_____

_____

_____

_____

_____

_____

_____

_____

_____

_____

Was there a time when my Grandma or Grandpa helped you in any way? How well did you know her or him, and how did it change your relationship?

_____

_____

_____

_____

_____

_____

_____

_____

_____

_____

_____

_____

_____

If you were to describe your favorite things about my grandparents, what would they be?

_____

_____

_____

_____

_____

_____

_____

_____

_____

_____

_____

_____

_____

[to your own parent(s)] What are one or two things that Grandma and Grandpa instilled in you that you felt were extremely important?

_____

_____

_____

_____

_____

_____

_____

_____

_____

_____

_____

_____

_____

When did you meet my Grandma and how?

_____

_____

_____

_____

_____

_____

_____

_____

_____

_____

_____

_____

_____

When did you meet my Grandpa and how?

_____

_____

_____

_____

_____

_____

_____

_____

_____

_____

_____

_____

What are some of the most special memories you have of my grandparents?

_ _

_ _

_ _

_ _

_ _

_ _

_ _

_ _

_ _

_ _

_ _

_ _

_ _

_ _

Is there anything they taught you that inspired you and you recall to this day?

_____

_____

_____

_____

_____

_____

_____

_____

_____

_____

_____

_____

_____

Was there a time when my Grandma or Grandpa helped you in any way? How well did you know her or him, and how did it change your relationship?

_____

_____

_____

_____

_____

_____

_____

_____

_____

_____

_____

_____

_____

_____

If you were to describe your favorite things about my grandparents, what would they be?

_____

_____

_____

_____

_____

_____

_____

_____

_____

_____

_____

_____

[to your own parent(s)] What are one or two things that Grandma and Grandpa instilled in you that you felt were extremely important?

_____

_____

_____

_____

_____

_____

_____

_____

_____

_____

_____

_____

"Grandma and Grandpa's Favorite Things"

From Grandma and Grandpa's favorite foods to their favorite places to travel, this section is a special reminder of their most treasured pastimes. Exploring each of these areas will be like opening a treasure chest. Your grandparents will certainly have a story to tell if you ask for more information about each of these. For example, don't just stop once they tell you the name of their favorite restaurant. Ask them more. Why do they like it so much? Was there one time that was more special than any other? Is that restaurant for occasions such as birthdays and anniversaries? Do the waiters know them by name? You can do a similar type of exploration for each of the questions. Have fun exploring!

If your grandparents are no longer with you, you can still fill out this section by asking other family members and friends. They will know and they will be happy to help you on your journey—asking them will also help them remember your Grandma and Grandpa one more time. That will be a treat for them!

Grandma's Leisure Time

Favorite hobby:

_____

_____

_____

_____

_____

_____

_____

_____

_____

_____

_____

_____

_____

Favorite holiday:

_____

_____

_____

_____

_____

Favorite way to pass the time:

_____

_____

_____

_____

_____

Favorite food for breakfast:

_____

_____

_____

_____

_____

_____

Favorite food for lunch:

_____

_____

_____

_____

_____

_____

Favorite food for dinner:

_____
_____
_____
_____
_____
_____

Favorite meal to make:

_____
_____
_____
_____
_____
_____

Least favorite food:

_____

_____

_____

_____

_____

_____

Favorite restaurant:

_____

_____

_____

_____

_____

_____

Person(s) you most admire:

_____

_____

_____

_____

_____

_____

Best advice you were ever given:

_____

_____

_____

_____

_____

_____

Favorite place(s) for a vacation:

_____

_____

_____

_____

_____

_____

Favorite movies:

_____

_____

_____

_____

_____

_____

Favorite musicals:

_____

_____

_____

_____

_____

_____

Favorite movie star:

_____

_____

_____

_____

_____

_____

Favorite television show when you were younger:

_____

_____

_____

_____

_____

_____

Favorite television show now:

_____

_____

_____

_____

_____

_____

Favorite radio show when you were younger:

_____

_____

_____

_____

_____

Favorite radio show now:

_____

_____

_____

_____

_____

Grandpa's Leisure Time
Favorite hobby:

_____

_____

_____

_____

_____

_____

_____

_____

_____

_____

_____

_____

_____

Favorite holiday:

_____

_____

_____

_____

_____

_____

Favorite way to pass the time:

_____

_____

_____

_____

_____

_____

Favorite food for breakfast:

_ _

_ _

_ _

_ _

_ _

Favorite food for lunch:

_ _

_ _

_ _

_ _

_ _

_ _

Favorite food for dinner:

_____

_____

_____

_____

_____

_____

Favorite meal to make:

_____

_____

_____

_____

_____

_____

Least favorite food:

_____

_____

_____

_____

_____

_____

Favorite restaurant:

_____

_____

_____

_____

_____

_____

Person(s) you most admire:

_____

_____

_____

_____

_____

_____

Best advice you were ever given:

_____

_____

_____

_____

_____

_____

Favorite place(s) for a vacation:

_____

_____

_____

_____

_____

_____

Favorite movies:

_____

_____

_____

_____

_____

_____

Favorite musicals:

_____

_____

_____

_____

_____

_____

Favorite movie star:

_____

_____

_____

_____

_____

_____

Favorite television show when you were younger:

_____

_____

_____

_____

_____

_____

Favorite television show now:

_____

_____

_____

_____

_____

_____

Favorite radio show when you were younger:

_____

_____

_____

_____

_____

_____

Favorite radio show now:

_____

_____

_____

_____

_____

_____

Around the World with Grandma and Grandpa
Places they have visited:

_____

_____

_____

_____

_____

_____

_____

_____

_____

_____

_____

_____

_____

_____

Friends they made while traveling:

_____

_____

_____

_____

_____

_____

_____

_____

_____

_____

_____

_____

_____

Memories from their favorite cities:

_____

_____

_____

_____

_____

_____

_____

_____

_____

_____

_____

_____

_____

Trips that were extra special:

_____

_____

_____

_____

_____

_____

_____

_____

_____

_____

_____

_____

_____

Special people/contacts Grandma and Grandpa want
their family to know:

_____

_____

_____

_____

_____

_____

_____

_____

_____

_____

_____

_____

_____

A Few Final Words

We hope that you have found this book to be very helpful. We know that many people don't have the pleasure of spending precious time with their grandparents. Whether it's distance, a broken relationship, or they are deceased, missing out on the joy of grandparents is a huge loss. If you used this book to gather more information about your Grandma and Grandpa, or if you are the grandparent who is recording information for future generations, the thoughts and discussions you had will become a significant part of shared memories. If this book has helped you have more discussions in your family, please leverage that and have more family talks—even casual ones will have a more special meaning to all of you.

Make the most of it. Before the day ends, tell someone in your family, "I love you" and continue to share the words that were lovingly recorded in this very special book. Keep in mind that time is a memory we must store in our hearts. By remembering and paying tribute to our loved ones, we allow them to live on forever.